Dear Reader

WE all live in OUR
own Universe
And in it **WE** are Gods
WE rule OUR
thoughts and emotions
Often times blinded by the Oceans
of Fate and hardships, pride and ego
until **WE** find OUR secret power
the weapon that outlasts time
_I_ listen to the poems wanting to
be written _I_ silence _my_ mind
and write the sounds of the
universe, the grey whispers and
buzzes that twitter in my ear
YOU are _my_ Boomerang,
Art finds its
way back to _me_
Harmed
Yet wanting more and
more pages
to be
filled and filled
Art needs a host
a body and a medium
WE are no better than
the bird decorating its
nest with flowers.
There is no better
there just
IS

MY MUSE

I love you

                                     as you keep me warm

At night

              filtering my dreams

Into rays of light

                                nourishing my soul

Awake

          you sing to me

                      as I listen and write

I feel complete

                            you make me whole

LOVE HEALS
VHY NOT DO IT MORE

As long as there are spirits in this world you
will never travel alone ♥

@LYDIAMUIJEN

UOY

SNOWFLAKE

In one exhale I stagger and when I open
my <u>eyes</u> and find myself in a dark
room with one small strip of <u>light</u> - the
yellow flowers and the Azure Cosmos
my sole <u>prize -</u> my Toes wiggle and
my Tummy smiles as <u>bright</u> as any
Golden Ornament.

The sounds are <u>silent</u> and the light is
quite black until I hear one <u>giggle,</u>
one tiny burst of laughter from out my
<u>window:</u> a child chasing a cricket.
The happiness <u>sprinkled</u> on top of our
steady and uneventful lives a tiny
flake that

OFFSETS

the whole

and sets all in motion

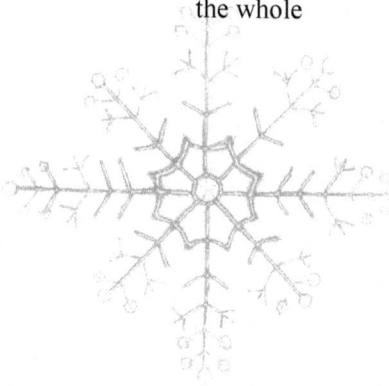

6

I ♥ U

I
LOVE
U
4
WHO
U
R
&
WHAT
U
DO
I
DO

I

♥

U

KRANE
I fold your forms
bend morph and change you into
something you were not
now you ARE
-a folded piece-
of paper and as I make
MORE
you become my peace pipe
my offering to
the others to find ways
to cross the barriers of
AGE and TIME
a little hand reaches up for her
-tiniest friend-
a "Tiny BiWd" for the other birds
to play with
a once unfolded piece of paper
now a spark of countless hours
of imagination to come

The LITTLE pink elephant
Love goes through your stomach into
the streets, water, or railway as you
<u>speed across</u> the world over land
or sea maybe even through the air
as you hop from **place to place**
Life is a routine that slides like the
BRIDGES carrying water over the
CANALS
and you stand
on one side looking at the people pass
effortlessly

like a little pink elephant scared to
follow in the footsteps of those who
went before

DIRTY FEET
Tread softly on the ground
as I watch your
STEPS
the dust moves and
clings to your
CELLS
as you tread the fool's
gold travels with you
I love your feet
No matter how many
Grains of pyrite
Cling to it

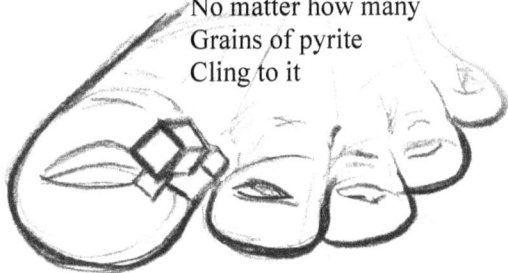

A breath of
Its a breath of fresh air
repeated time and time again
when you love someone fair
and their heart you obtain

love is all that is needed
to bridge the gap of time
a sickness when untreated
merges souls in silly rhyme
a kind gesture or a smile
patience will get versatile

love is the lightning when it thunders
it heals and in time performs wonders

I See No More

The moon lights up my longing for your
touch I breathe you in as I quiver for
your embrace blood flows in my veins
as a river that had much rain and as I
swell **hard** TIME keeps enslaved

I would give up my life as I know it in a
blink of an EYE. I see you near me
together again! Yet when you are near I
hesitate and shrink. My soul prays to
keep this feeling without end.

I scent your soul near mine; I light up
Like the Olympian flame burning ever
longer I swell and overflow my being. I
erupt; I give in to you and fall with joy
and laughter

Rolling, tumbling now on the floor. I lay
with you. I look feel open my eyes and
see no more. I move away and love
remains. Desire has fled and proven
pointless

With you I know "I am"
your hands reach out and touch my heart
with you my cells turn into soil
You can mold me move me
grateful to be farmed upon

I feel myself change as if some
stagnant water turning into a spring
I like who I become
through your touch
The world becomes clearer

And I learn how to move
I lay still

Still, I dance with you

All the castles in the world will
not buy the way you make me feel

With you I feel "I am" and "in being"
I know to move - yet not sure how

True love
I see your eyes
and yet you are not here
you pierce at me through
the darkness
Two blue orbs
brighten my room
and as I open my
eyes I feel your touch
traveling back
I live again in a moment
past
future and present
merge and become
one as I come
to the realization
that time does not
exist

The Greater
You are great as you smile
from ear to ear and
Radiate JOY to others
your moon in LEO
meant to perform to
Spit and heal through
your ART and PASSION
while you travel the world
wrapped in bacon and ready

- for any good cause

Down to an Azure Sea
Now remember the risks taken
and the safe steps on the road
past the faces
masked and miraculous
one sees one
and one knows the other
or maybe not

spirits know all
but cannot materialize
unless given the power
yet I wish I had known and listened
to those spirits

AMONG US they LIVE

they live in a **thought** and in a **shiver**,
but never too present

life has ended as we know it

and before it ends learn to be a better
man

HOTTUBSUMMIT
SUNDANCE SLAMDANCE STEAM
steams up from the HOTTUB
as they are having a SUMMIT
in PARK CITY in the SNOW

My wrists lean on the icy metal
to cool off as the Camera's
film the film makers share
some fun film makingfacts

Ice can be desired in a tub
that is too hot for most it
would melt the *ice man* it
is almost European to have

naked people in the snow
some places it is considered
normal COLD is good for your
immune system and is **THE KEY**
to master your inner core

HA CHI I SNEEZE allergic to the
nano particles in the air I train
my CHI to rise TAI CHI CHI GONG
and what not self control through
ICE and SNOW in a steaming
hot TUB

SLAMDANCE

My paradise
I close my eyes for
you are my paradise
the silence between words
and thoughts cease
when you are near
Life is hell but not
as long as YOU are in
it whereever you go
in spirit I will follow
step by step in the
SHADOWS I remain
like the phantom at
the Garnair living
at a distance until

the bell tolls for me

SKUNK

FEARLESS

      - you explore the night

WATCHING

      - creatures sleep

on a BIG BED surrounded
by *dichotemous* EARTH in
an attempt to keep the critters

OUT

You always have felt welcome

OUTSIDE

      - in nature

UNTIL

      you jumped in bed with:

2 HUMANS

How could they have known!

That you just like to STARE

and to watch them sleep?

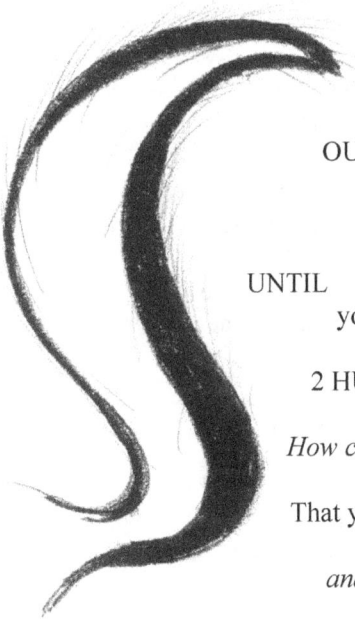

17

MUSES move at CYCLING speed

My <u>thoughts</u> move at the *speed* of **light**
As I cycle past **concrete** and **asphalt**
The sand glistens in the light of the
setting sun as I speed past the TREES
Too slow for cars I shift gears
the **MUSES** are catching up with me
as everyone **Waxes** their ears to not hear
the **SIRENS** sing their *silent* **song**

I <u>think</u> of you and in that thought
I am with you - in your presence -
and wonder if all is well.
I <u>think;</u> therefore, I move.
beyond myself into realms
of the unknown. I see and in the
reflection of the outside world is the
never ending **RECURSION** of oneself.

We are the fractals ever shrinking
within itself as the rest EXPANDS we
move inward unless we look beyond
OUR*selves* and step out of what we
<u>think</u> and **feel** and <u>focus</u> on the one that
is right there next to us.

The *homeless* man on the street, the
child playing across the field, your
neighbour giving a helping hand. How
do they **feel**; what do they <u>think</u>?
Move speak and **BE** with whoever is
next to you and share. Share how they

make you **feel**. Appreciate an "other"
and in that lose YOUR*self.*

And in losing yourself; you find who
you truly are. Without <u>thought</u> without
feeling in the silence of what **IS**.

Birth

Miles away you
have
Made a miracle
A tiny person
with DNA all
Twisted right
A perfect little
creature
Loved by all who
clap eyes on
The smiling
Buddha
you made me a
friend
A new soul to
give life
More meaning

Bird house

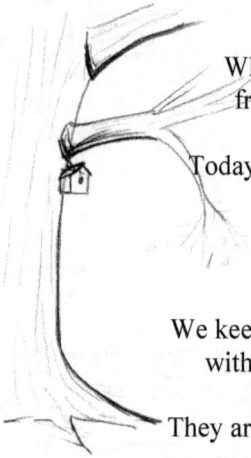

What we can do is different
from what we want to do.

Today you could build a home for
someone.

It is simple.

We keep our homes clean and sterile,
with no space for bird or beast.

They are forced to "invade" our home
just like we did theirs.

Yet, today like many others
people built homes across the world
for birds of all sizes.

They need some shelter from rain
a hole small enough to protect them
from predators in a shaded space
that hides them from plain sight.

SUNNY side

Bright and shiny
most radiant **SELF**
Strong
in your course
inside
fragile and small
Protected by
the light
from those
who wish you harm
Inner beauty is seen
by the ones
who can look
into the
SUN

EM

I LOST MYSELF

I am afraid I might have lost myself.
but then again
"you cannot really be lost;
you have to be
'somewhere'"
- or so the *BUSHMEN* say

EXHALE
I open my
SOUL
and let **it** out
the hurt
the sorrow
and give it back
to the UNIVERSE
As things flow I shout
silently and

collapse

In the Water
legs and feet move
at the same time
with their fiery bellies
they burn my skin
as I rinse off the
POISON
from the oak
I lay still silently
listening to the sounds
of the leaves and the chanting
of the birds contemplating to sleep
inside
our concrete
PRISONS
or to sleep
outside on the soft mossy
altar of the bears and mountain lions
STUCK
in limbo I remain motionless
burning from head to toe

IF I HAD A MILLION DOLLARS

If I had a million dollars I would sing
with you, play with you, clean up
garbage with you and do the dishes with
you.

If I had a million dollars I would give it
all to you - and some to a charity - and
maybe some to buy some chocolate to
SHARE of course

If I had a million dollars I would
refurbish and insulate a woodshed and
build an extra large bed with a fireplace
to keep ME warm - YOU will probably
be warm already - so just in case.

If I had a million dollars I would buy
you a boat with a fire extinguisher and
an e-purp - so you could sail to the
Caribbean if you wanted to

If I had a million dollars I would love to
buy me a job a really nice one to keep
me busy - for YOUR sake If I had a
million dollars I would love to hear you
snore, but then again I feel like a million
dollars every time I am with you

GOD'S GIFT   to   ME

I see but **MY** eyes trap **MY** soul
and keep **ME** from YOU.
I restrain **MY***self* and keep **MY***self* from
YOU **MY** dear dear heart
I long for YOU yet
I run from YOU
I keep **MY***self* away with the immense
desire to protect YOU from myself
I love you more then **MY** own dear self
I would gladly give **MY***self* away for
YOUr gain
I would place
MY hands under YOUr feet
not for submission or crazy folly for
I know
MY hands will be safe in YOUrs
I worry **_not_** about what the world feels
or thinks
All **I** know is that YOU exist in **IT** and
that gives **MY** life its meaning

YOU are god's gift to **ME**.

THUNDER
The sky turns dark blue
purple and green.
Inside all the electronics are being
unplugged from walls.
Computers and phones
to protect them,
to save them
from the blue flashes
that jump trough space
connecting one wall socket
with the other.
As the air turns static,
the Clouds roar
I count between
the rumble and the flashes:
One, two, three,
as the dog hides under the table.
One, two,
FLASH even closer!
I am on a wooden chair
Not aligned with wall sockets or
electronics as the house has become the
god's jittergame hoping they will not
            Bring the ball
                    I patiently wait
                            One strike
flash
            rumble and silence
                    all goes black
Thunder is nature's warning of what is
to come - As I light my candle and
fireplace - no more wifi
Thank the GODS for books

ONE DAY

one day I will be happy
one day I will be glad

one day I will look in the mirror
without feeling sad

one day I might grow a smile
one day I might be happy
if only for a while

one day I will learn to surf
spend hours on the beach
with inner joy and mirth :)

my thoughts will cease
-- if you will, please! --

upon a bank of sand
one day I will rest my head
and find something to befriend

a gentle breeze now blows on me
my cells dispersing in the wind
my ashes off to sea

one day I will fall in laughter
one day I will jump with joy

and move to somewhere grander
if it is the last thing that I'll do

for now I will keep on breathing
'nd take it one step at a time

♡ **Annie MG Schmidt**

thank god for rhyme and reason

what's past I can't undo now
it is sad but -- oh -- so true

Poets speak about the present
the great HERE and NOW
I wish I had not lost it

I wish I could loop back in time
but I don't know how

one day I will build an igloo
'nd run around in the snow

one day birds will land on me
and I will be still as ice
happily rooted as a tree
I will be their paradise

OUTSIDE
I see myself as I lay still
silently starving
Yet unable to move
I listen to the rhythmic beat
of the traffic
the high-pitched noise
of the electrical humming
unable to hear my own heart beat
The busy hummingbird happily
flying from flower to flower
as I stare out of my window
contemplating to move or to get up and
make something out of myself
and the remainder of my life
as people freshen their faces
with stem cells and
INSTAGRAM their lives

The food I eat makes me swell up
like a frightened Pufferfish
I prefer to stay to not move or eat
until a *butterfly* comes to my window-
the BIGGEST one I have ever seen.
On my flight outside
I take the lens cap off
vaguely remembering the sense of loss
now outside in pursuit of nature
to admire and to LOVE

Grateful
I woke up
to find I grew
myself
a new heart
Today
U
GREW
myself
a new heart
I get up and watch the moon
get fuller
and fuller
until the light
hits
me and
I see
I see and feel my light
grow with the beams
and the indirect sunlight
reflected off of you
I saw the sun
but could not grow
from it.

The sun's light was
too bright
I would shrivel
lose my leaves
My dear moon
your seed
nurtured my heart and
my soul
is growing still

I feel
I love
and live
lost
I had given up hope
hope to live
and love again
and still my mind
wants
me not to
give in to love
and life
but I find myself
living again

as I love
the moon
the rocks
the people
Dear moon
I love you
for you gave me
back my soul
and self again

Paradise is upstream
You won't believe it,
but I found it the other day, you see

A kind stranger showed me the way.
At the unpruned oak we scared a quail
from its nest.

I climb up to the still stream past the
boulders and the rocks.

On the back of the dragon,
its rough skin warming my bony self.

In fairy lands I sit and watch the newts
play: training to fly.

Irony
I wanted a life of tradition
I but jumped into an adventure
I ended up in solitude
But scream for some affection

WOMAN DIARIES

click click click click

the clapping of the rocks in the hands of
MEN
men who lust for blood and RELIGION

cars and sunglasses

my verdict is DEATH
and JUSTICE

honor will return in a town

saved by a circus

a sign of   G O D

to stop the stoning

men cheer longing for death

my grave ready to bury my chaste bones

I stand
alone amidst
my peers my town

- the time has come

MOVING ON

With eyes as bright as snow
and a smile that outshines the sun
I see you

my time is fleeting on this earth
and writing seems to make things last
scraps of paper thoughts and words
all together built my past

I reach deep to find some wit
to build a rhyme and have it sit
like ink drying on an untouched quill
unmoved and sticky it remains quite still

Mister, keep the heart you stole
it might do someone good one day
the lies and hurt went down the hole
I found some friends less dark and grey

NO NEED TO PANIC !
Higher means no and dirt is not soil
4 a number

the sounds are the same
yet all means something other than what
you or me might think

I travel and find people are the same
they laugh they hurt they grow and learn
and forget sometimes

things that seem
so different are quite the same

I drink my Chai and find that taking
my shoes off at my home makes
sense in some places.

Where the bus stops after it passes the
stop and where jaywalking is the norm.

SAMSUN
Less worry
more life
where boardgames are
done in the street
families
spend time
<u>without</u>
their computers
and phones

Time ticks
we miss most of it

                except when we travel.

The electricity
falls out
in the airport
no one reacts
            this type of thing is normal:

Things happen
that is life.

IN THE LAST DEGREE

And the verdict is
in the last degree
<u>hungry</u>
<u>thirsty</u>
reason to guide
our lost souls
as we play *dress-up*
masked from our true selves and scared
to LIVE
we hurt the ones we love and
turn the whole world into an
army of meaningless zombies

as the night falls we hear the screams
from the cemetery
we cannot turn back **time**
and they know it
drowning in regret they linger on

Time does not exist for those who are
Lost and yet for the ones who live time
ticks ticks ticks as an endless drip that
makes way for a stream

HE BECKONS ME

My heavy lids long for you as
My brain becomes a mush
my nymphs beckon me to our bed
HYPNOS thy wish is my command
I am married to you for half my life and
gladly close my eyes to spend it with
you – soundly asleep
As I fall down the rabbit hole I am
connected tuned into the grid, or the
Universe as we used to call it. You show
me my lost loved ones untill I am
woofully woken by the alarm.
I climb back up to consciousness and as
I struggle I forget about you for 12
hours or so, untill you send your MUSE
to fetch me back to you

I HIDE in YOU
I sleep
in my dreams
you are with me
and I am with you
as I awaken
you disappear and my soul reaches out
for you
as you slowly vanish in my mind's eye.
I drown in sadness
for my loss of the person
I could have been with you.
Alone
comfortable
covered
I curl up and close my eyes
forcing a smile
Hypnos take me away
untill I can
smile
again.

Glasses
Designer fashionable glasses
Borrowed taken
Now broken
I am left with the pieces
Of your wear
Shards bring luck they say
As I stare
Thinking about glue
Or some solution
Unable to decide I learn
To appreciate its pieces
First there was one pair
Of …
And now there are many
Pieces

MAGNAcarta
Movies are getting shorter as our
attention span decreases
Time is ticking faster in this world
where there is room for the fast and
furious, but those who long to be
OFF
The grid
Are having trouble fitting in
The Zombies are taking over
Ruining the plan as only lovers are left
alive with no clean blood to eat

KINDness

KINDness = priceless
In a world that seems
lost and hopeless

I smile as I look around
The man who can eat toast
only; he has a budget
The girl who cannot eat;
her stomach is upset

Grateful for KINDness
In a world full of people

who are KIND - sometimes-
in a world that seems a mess

FREE - to change
FREE - to grow
FREE - to share a moment

and let some KINDness
GROW

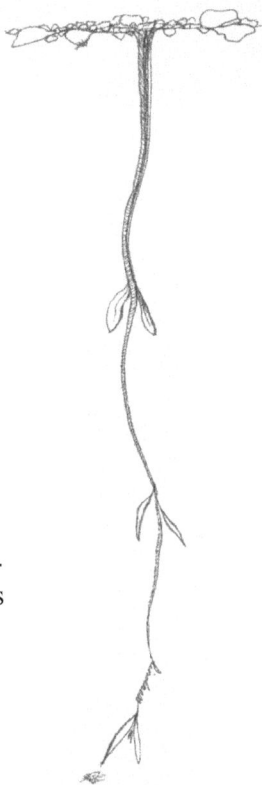

SU

The Crow was Crowing on the shore
When HUMAN BEINGS found **their**
existence would come to end,
They sent a **RAVEN** up to the skies with
a message:

*"we want clean water to drink and land
to live on. We do not want to live on
deserts and oceans floating and
wandering without a solid home."*

Instead the **OCEANS** rose and **SOIL**
turned into **SAND**. Struggling to adjust
to **their** desert planet. REpenting
REgretting SOULLESS BEINGS
begging creatures for a **SPACE**.

They wished for **FORESTS** filled with
FRUIT. OCEANS filled with **LIFE**
and **MEADOWS** crawling with
TOADS.

Promising the SKIES to change **their**
ways. Yet the SKIES and HUMANS
took second place the **RAVEN** in its
flight found a sparkling PIECE of
PLASTIC. In its dive down to the
deserted shore **IT** picked up the JEWEL
and looked for a **PLACE** to store and
keep the GEM.

And that is when the WATERBEAR
went up and reached the SKIES. The

WATERBEAR that heard the wailing of the HUMANS. First said HUMANS want water to become HEAVY and loaded with TAR. They want oceans as acidic as COKE and the **EARTH** as hot as a SAUNA.

Then the sky saw the CORAL dissolve as the *CO2* took the SHELLS away. The souls of the plankton and the dying species joined in the SKY in the HEAVENS while the souls of the HUMANS melted and Radiated into the ACID of the TAR-filled **OCEANS** as they witnessed how they changed a lush HEAVEN into a HELL.

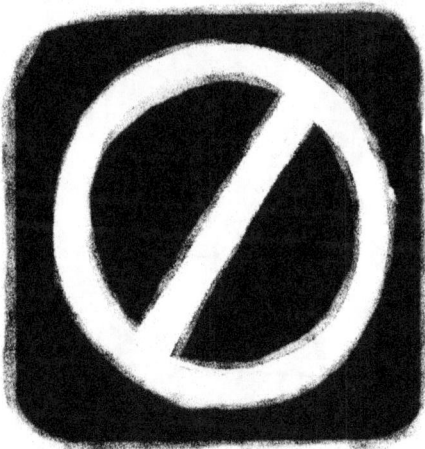

You tell me!
How like a web we are interwoven
You pull; I move.
I fall; you stumble.
You hurt; I cry.
I love; you smile
quietly each sting pulls us closer.

There is no direct path in life;
or so it seems as we flip like
pinball balls.

Moths and flies cross our path:
We stretch;
or get **stuck**;
or eaten;
or leave

Is
LIFE
a web we entangle ourselves in
or it it the **STRING** that makes
the spider cross rivers

Be With me in Silence
Be with me in silence, motionless and
still. Oh me what silence has your
LOVE put on my lips? I cease to **feel** *as*
I absorb your being and lose
myself.

Now, lost I try to find the
Missing Piece
The Glue
to tie things back together again. Yet, I
just see the sound between the spaces;
and as I listen to the LIGHT- words lose
their meaning.

I attempt to think a thought but the
wheels are not TURNING inside my
mind.
I ask you to be silent with me
to cease
All Being   -   *All Feeling*
and in
THAT SPACE
you can be with me
inert
inactive and
STILL
In any other SPACE you will find me
lost, searching, falling down and in that
I cease to be until you HALT and give
me
R O O M
to grow *Breathe* and
b e   s t i l l

THE MISSING SPIDER

Your first thought when you feel the
tearing sounds as you open the door is
"I destroyed something" Your eyes
dance to find the origin of the vibrations
but part of your mind wants to shut the
door
                                    - To hide -
from the eyes that might hover in
judgement from its now destroyed nest
Still you dare to investigate and inspect
the woven ruin in the top of the left
corner like cameras the eyes record your
every movement how would you battle
something that size. *Do you give it a
chance?* To walk away from the fight;
so you can save your soul?
Something that smart and delicate and
powerful, Must have been put in that
corner for a reason!

A carcass floating in a web clearly a
creature that can battle something 4
times its size MUST be left alone!
Still! The body must be saved from this
shadowy creature with ALL SEEING
eyes.

This was a very big and ugly spider web
Is all you can say to your roommate as
You exit from the back door of the
house A swoop and smash is heard as
you walk around the house

"Two dead spiders, but no living one I found"

LIZARD
My truant friend what sees your spirit
soul? You look and raise yourself to **me**
And expose your bright blue kept **secret**
I find you silent and in that you are set
free.

Connected we find a way to pause our
thoughts Your beauty camouflaged
against a **tree;** browns and greys dance
while I sit and eat and **squat** Beside you
under the sun on my arbourous **bench**

I learn one lesson after the other by
being by just being and no more. My
pround **teacher**. Patiently waiting for
me to leave your **home** showing your
presence by flowing up and **down** the
branches.

While I have a friendly **picnic** your
spirit will outlive my soul as you **glide**
through time, eternal invisible timeless
and **still**

WE STARE
You have the choice to LOOK and
SMILE and as you **SHINE** you pull out
mine as my face stretches and contorts
the SKIN pulling and showing my
TEETH

You have the choice to STARE at your
SCREEN or to go outside and watch a
TREE grow a kid play or a gardener
mow you can learn a new language or
do something **NEW**

You have the choice to keep staring at
that SCREEN of yours those bits and zeros
of LCD or OLED vibrating light into
your **RETINA**

I stare and stare deep into Plato's
shadows

I have the choice to let go and **MOVE**
from one thing to another. To stop
Sitting STILL and to **MOVE** and feel as
my body **SMILES** with the thought I
wiggle my toes in excitement.

We live in caves and stare at WALLS
focused and lost we cannot control our
thoughts and emotions and are led and
controlled but not by ourselves love or
kindness

- we just follow -

We have a choice to stand up and **LIVE**
or sit STILL and STARE

ICED people
Control your self
Your breath
MASTER
All
Feel your cells your skin
And organs get fuel
Throught each inhalation
As you burn your sadness
You sit in ice and force that
ENGINE of yours
To kick in driving your body
Downhill to get a kickstart
INDIGOGO
For your body as you
Go into the bath of ice
To find your new
OLD
you

HUMANS

The twittering leaves that fall and get
replaced through the ages
DNA gets shorter and shorter like the
stories of our past
We discover things over and over again
as our
Mutual consciousness grows and shrinks
at the same time
we stir our tea as we did years ago
click click click click click

drip drip

click

and now we read our papers and stare at
our screen
and forget the customs and traditions
and
our families who sit across us from the
table
<u>yet we see them not.</u>

The journey starts **within** slowly
shedding
peeling the onion layer for layer
until we finally find ourselves

ENOUGH

My eyes stare yet I see not and
my lungs refuse to inhale I
force air in and out
in and out
as my eyes had enough

Enough of today and the external
stimuli of sounds and colors
new thoughts make way for
silence and the colors morph
into darkness

as everything becomes light as a feather
and I float away somewhere
where there is no me
                somewhere
where there is no us
                    somewhere

where there only   **IS**

and that is enough

MR RIGHT SIDE UP

LOVE IS
LOVE is not about knowing truth.
It is not about asking questions or
                                    - knowing facts
LOVE is the love of a father for his
child even when it is not his own.
LOVE is about the silent affection for a
friend. *LOVE* is the forgiveness that
comes from being human. *LOVE* does
not find faults or imperfections:

love sees the whole painting and picture
from the right angle in the proper light
like the artist meant for it to be seen;
not through a looking glass or through
an x-ray or taken apart.

LOVE, art and nature are ONE a whale
swimming free in the oceans is not
less pure than the most worshipped
work of art. *LOVE* is allowing life and
freedom without intervention; without
limitation; with acknowledgment.

LOVE is not seeing the world in its
entire form, but it is the fabric of every
atom woven and strung together in one
giant canvas.
We live in the *Garden of Earth* and its
resources are meant to be nurtured
and *LOVED* not taken studied and
dissected.

To study a poet is not to drug kill it and
then put it under a microscope. The
study of nature should be the same.
Learn to *LOVE* like the love of a mother
for her child.
Learn to *LOVE* those who cannot and
above all *SMILE,*
smile like your day depends on it and
                                        who knows
you might give someone a glimpse of
HOPE and brighten their day

Return from the Muses
The clock glides
as the seconds become
LONGER
the muffled sounds
now in the background
As I transform and teleport
ELSEWHERE
My body
FROZEN
yet able to travel space and time
to be with you
my love
you let me
You see me
SHIFT
and you give me the
RIGHT
to be
ELSEWHERE
with you
my brain
the wormhole people look for
I travel back home
The world is asleep
I no longer in it
MY SPACESHIP
safe in your presence
as you shelter IT from harm.
My dear dear friend I am your ALIEN
your ELF
As I come back
bit by bit
I smile

HAPPY
to be back with you
in a cloud of tinkling inspiration
in the middle
of your couch

I choose you
I want your happiness over mine
I want you worry-free and blessed

I want you safe and sound

Your presence means the world to me
yet, not if my being bothers you

I long to touch caress and hold you
but not if you desire someone else

I would love to grow old with you
spend time with you cook for you

watch things grow with you
I choose you - please choose too

SILENT TIME
You make time
STOP
your touch moves
ME
back in time and as you play
I become MY*self* for a moment
past present and future
ARE

1

WE are the bridge
floating in space   connecting
NOTHING
but
our true selves
and as we come
CLOSE
MY skin against YOURS
we border one another never able to
CROSS

2

countries at peace
WE see each other
and love one another
for what we are
Unable to move further we lay
Smiling
HAPPY
as the world moves around US
WE remain frozen
timeless and still
pulled   away
we grow further

60

APART
yet in the distance we find
ourselves
1
connected through some
STRINGS
merging close yet oh so far
in peace with FATE
we live **1** day
at a time
&
as long as you are in
it
I smile

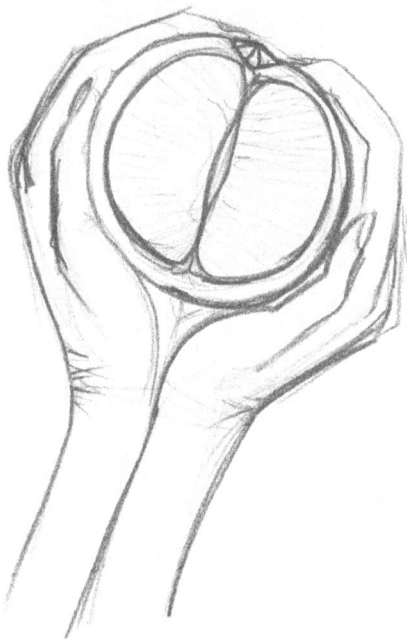

ZORK
I have a dream that one day I will ...
*what mom yes mom I will mom I
will be right there mom yes thank
you mom*

I have a dream that one day I will rise
my to my ...

yes yes yes

wait a minute

where was I. I was ... oh yeah that was
it

I have a dream that one day I will find
the girl who would have and bury and
wrap a **dozen children** with **me.**

Unless of course she does not want to
have children.

I will have whatever she wants to have.

It will be perfect.

"Zork!"

Dancing with the LEAVES
LIFE
STILL
SOLID and beating
we move from leaf to leave
as we flip pages though
time connecting verse by
verse I write in your footsteps
and rhyme in your shadow
NEVER ALONE
your words with me as the
Muses sing with the night'gale out
yonder window. I smile as I close my
eyes as I know your winged syllables
have taken flight and charmed many

I will write and will live - for you will
be in it

The ELEMENTS
hitting and *caressing* me
I learn where I begin and the world ends
in real TIME as the imaginary numbers
move perpendicular

We are able to cross SPACE in ways we
never thought possible our minds
connecting, communication with our
PAST & FUTURE
in the moment surrounded by the
ATOMS
that spark our cells - in an ever
expanding UNIVERSE

Words fall short
one by one
on your way home
flown
carried
we lift you
in silence
we give you peace
rest and room
now that life has been
taken from you
we want to give you love
peace in a world full of
hate and war
we love you
and all of you
together
in a disaster
carried back home
We are silent for you
and we grant you so much more
we are stunned and still
one by one
on your way home

HOPE FOR YOU
I have hope for you
as you shed your skin
your cells
growing and expanding
with the universe
you grow and live and learn
I would wish for the world to heal
but there is war in learning
wiring, twisting and relearning habits
the world exists not because it is
PEOPLED
A tree that *longs* to grow has just as
much *desire* and will to live as an ant or
ape!
There are smart people, like dolphins
and there are dumb people like
HOMO SAPIENS
all roaming this planet
Some animal keen on
Being
others keen on
HAVING
OBTAINING & CONQUERING
all the same
A mom can love her child
a dog can love its owner
why can't all HUMANS learn to love

MANGOSTEEN
Your peel - your cover -
Is strong *yet soft* to touch
My fingers glide over your *skin*
As you dangle and fall
Now in my hand I find a way
To open you up and as you break
I smell your *sweet* scent as
The molecules torpedo into my nostrils
Your white mushy inside melt
In my mouth. I found you downtown
My rare forbidden fruit

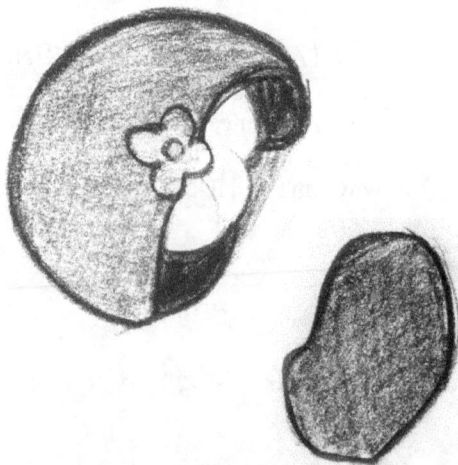

Lydia Muijen's first poetry collection "25 & 25 couples and more" was published in 2010. Two of her poems have been selected as poem of the week in Australia for *OZPOETRY SOCIETY*: "Teach me" and "I think I love you." Additionally, two poems one called "Why not do it more" and the other "Tweet Twitter Twat" were published in an Australian poetry magazine *THE CURIOUS RECORD*. As a poet she has received requests to write for radio. In 2012 she wrote "Zombieland" for ADRENALINE radio. Additionally, for the last 2 years Lydia has written en recited poems for *FACETS OF THE HEART* – an online weekly radio show based in Los Angeles, California. "Love Heals" is a collection of some of her most recent poems.

CONTENTS/INDEX:

LOVE HEALS VHY NOT DO IT MORE

**PUBLISHER: NAU UITGEVERS P.O. 146,
1260AC BLARICUM, THE NETHERLANDS**
WWW.NEDERLANDSEAUTEURSUITGEVERIJ.NL

LITERARY AGENT AND FOREIGN RIGTHS:
NEDERLANDS AUTEURS BUREAU, BLARICUM
THE NETHERLANDS. WWW.AUTEURSBUREAU.NL

First Edition January 2015

A SPECIAL THANK TO DR. G. M. MOORE
And a special thanks my family and friends ♥

COVER AND DESIGNS BY LYDIA MUIJEN

NUR: 306
ISBN : 9789491535 284

ALSO AVAILABLE IN DIGITAL VERSIONS
NUR: 306
ISBN : 9789491535 277